Butterfly Matrix

A Daily Planner and Workbook for a More Positive Life

Angela Gerber

BALBOA.
PRESS

A DIVISION OF HAY HOUSE

Editing by Shellie Keller and Angela Gerber

Balboa Press books may be ordered through booksellers or by contacting:

Balboa Press
A Division of Hay House
1663 Liberty Drive
Bloomington, IN 47403
www.balboapress.com
1 (877) 407-4847

Because of the dynamic nature of the Internet, any web addresses or links contained in this book may have changed since publication and may no longer be valid. The views expressed in this work are solely those of the author and do not necessarily reflect the views of the publisher, and the publisher hereby disclaims any responsibility for them.

The author of this book does not dispense medical advice or prescribe the use of any technique as a form of treatment for physical, emotional, or medical problems without the advice of a physician, either directly or indirectly. The intent of the author is only to offer information of a general nature to help you in your quest for emotional and spiritual well-being. In the event you use any of the information in this book for yourself, which is your constitutional right, the author and the publisher assume no responsibility for your actions.

Any people depicted in stock imagery provided by Thinkstock are models, and such images are being used for illustrative purposes only.
Certain stock imagery © Thinkstock.

ISBN: 978-1-4525-8737-0 (sc)
ISBN: 978-1-4525-8738-7 (e)

Printed in the United States of America.

Balboa Press rev. date: 01/08/2014

Dedication:

This book is dedicated to Bess Wintrich; a woman that inspired the part of me that urges to heal others, to Goldie; my guardian angel who spoke and guided me to through life in the right direction through butterflies, and to all my friends and family who stood by my side and believed in me. I will never forget you.

Contents

Preface

If there was a daily planner that not only had space for you to write down things you must do on your "day to day", but also gave you the space to learn how to introduce more positivity into your life; would you take a second look or would you say, "Nope I like being in constant negative chaos"?

Deep in each of our souls we want to learn how to be more positive and know how it affects our body every time we do. We want to know how to create that sacred space where people can just leave us alone and we focus on nothing but our passions. We want to be able to read a meditation that brings us back to a positive state in an instant when a boss, coworker, friend, or husband/wife makes us angry! We want to write our biyearly intentions and gratitude's to remind us what our true goal is.

Last but not least, we want to have all this included with our "day to day" planner because my friend; it is a part of our plan entirely. All of this combined helps keep us responsible for not only picking up the dry cleaning, but doing it with a smile. You will be a step ahead in more ways than most and that is passion for yourself my friend. Either you embrace it or you continue to be on the tread mill.

My choice was to walk away from the treadmill and now I am bringing the option and chance to change life for you. When I was a young woman my grandmother told me that she was a healer in World War 2. She taught me to heal and I have been trying to heal individuals my entire life now. She died of cancer when I was barely 17 years old. I wanted to create something to make her proud and donate a portion of the net profit to help make individuals with dis-eases have a happier life. I believe that is the real cure; happiness. This book is about 15 years in the making and I never gave up the desire to create it. It is the start of my life's work and I love it. Now it is complete and my hope is that it helps you as much as it has saved me.

Introduction

The Butterfly Matrix begins with an explanation of what the Butterfly Matrix is and then on to the designer guide explaining how to utilize certain parts of the planner/work book. After this it goes into how to create your sacred space.

Creating your sacred space helps you find a specific area just for you to find your peace. It can be used for meditation, yoga, or even just filling out your Butterfly Matrix work book.

We then go into positive thinking and meditations. Here you learn how to think positive and why it is important to think positive, while providing you with some unique meditations to bring you balance. Both of these sections help center you and empty your mind of thoughts that do not serve you, in order to move forward with clear head.

Biannual intentions and gratitude lists are next. These are fun because on the intentions you get to write down what you intend for your life for six months of the year, and the gratitude lists remind you of all the things you already have to be grateful for already. It has been said that showing gratitude for what you already have brings more into your life.

Finally we have the daily planner. Just like any other daily planner, you use it for writing down your day to day activities. If you have a new idea, goal, or inspirational quote you find, you can also write it down. The daily planner helps keep track of not just your "day to day" life; it helps you keep track of your spiritual life as well.

The Butterfly Matrix is designed to help you reach a new height in your life. It can be the journal that helps shape your life, and all you have to do is write it down.

What is the Butterfly Matrix?

The Butterfly Matrix is the chaos of all things in existence. Using the Butterfly Matrix as a tool can reveal the world as it is, one gigantic wave of vibration that it truly is. We use the term "vibration" because that is exactly what everything is. Movement that is created by energy and that is responsible for everything that exists. There is energy in everything that exists: the chair, that pillow sitting next to you, all organic beings, and everything.

Energy creates vibration and vibration creates a frequency. Thought is a frequency created by energy from this vibration. This frequency ("thought") is carried through the body, carried through the field around the body (also called the "aura"), and carried all throughout the field of the universe.

In the past it was believed that thought was only a random chemical reaction from neurons firing in the brain and that was it. Thought is not just part of a separate "one" body reaction though. Thoughts (being that they are frequencies) are coming from other energy fields (other people's energy fields) because there is no such thing as separate energy fields; everything is operating in one giant energy field and everything is connected. Therefore, it is important to only allow the thoughts that serve you and throw away the thoughts that do not.

All organic beings (organisms that are alive) have a soul. The soul is the "energy spirit" created by the energy that is behind all things that exist. The soul enters into an organic being and life is created. The combination of this soul and the organic being's heart creates a unique frequency for that specific being. This is where we get our individuality and our individual emotions that are created in this organic being from this heart soul frequency combination.

The heart is the ruler of the body and emanates the largest electrical magnetic signal in the body. It rules over all the systems, organ, and cells of the body. The heart receives outside stimulation faster than the brain, relays it to the brain, and then it is relayed to the rest of the body.

Energy cardiology today is telling us that the signals produced by the heart are important for regulatory. The heart is continually emitting heat, light, electrical magnetic signals, and pressure waves. All systems, organs, and cells are receiving all of these different signals at different times. The reason for this is because they travel at different speeds through the circulatory system. So there is not only blood flowing through your veins, there is information!

Magnetic fields are like waves and the magnetic wave that flows to the heart, to the brain, and then throughout the body is a carrier wave of information. Information is what is being imprinted on each carrier wave. If we are feeling love towards a person or situation there is a very different imprint than if there is hate and despair. The hearts coherent rhythm (smooth pattern from love, peace, and harmony) and incoherent rhythm (unsmooth patterns from anger and despair) trains the brain and rest of the body to this synchronized rate.

Knowing and understanding this process you can change a negative disposition into a positive position. In the Butterfly Matrix there may be chaos with waves of frequencies with information flying everywhere and the thought of this massive amounts of information could be scary, but don't let frighten you. There is such a thing of complete peace with in the matrix of it all. You just have to have heart coherence in connection with your wings while flying on the waves.

Designer Guide

How to use the Butterfly Matrix Daily Planner and Workbook:

(1. **The Diet**)- Every day, write down on your daily planner what and when you eat daily to keep track of your intake.

(2. **Meditation**)- Meditation includes the meditation of physical meditation and mental meditation. Physical meditation is referred to as body exercise and stretching. Mental exercise is referred to as meditation of the mind (calming your mind of all outside distractions), and working on your gratitude lists. Plan and write in on your daily planner a time you can allow yourself these meditations for that day. It is important to the natural flow of your body to spend <u>at least</u> 15 minutes a day raising your heart beat in exercise, and then spending <u>at least</u> 15 minutes a day to empty your mind from those thoughts that do not serve you (bringing your mind to a peaceful state). Another wonderful thing to incorporate into your morning and night plans is stretching. Stretching not only increases flexibility which strengthens the tendons; it ultimately strengthens the muscles in the body as well. So the three things to remember to incorporate into your daily plan is exercise, stretching, and meditating.

(3. **Positive Thinking**)- Positive thinking is a way to stay "up-beat", understand interactions with others when they are not as positive, and how to receive the best experience from those interactions. Be positive in a negative situation and you will continue to have a bright and shiny day.

(4. **Gratitude List**)- "For yourself, your life, and others that exist in your experience." In this book there are 13 pages of gratitude lists. When something in your experience comes your way and you are grateful for it, write down these things on the gratitude lists so that you can remember why life is wonderful to you.

(5. **Biannual Intentions**)- This is a special section for you to write down your intentions. You do this when you first receive this book and during the six months you use it. Intentions are your plans, hopes, and dreams. What do you intend to experience in your life? Write your intentions and begin creating them.

Sacred Space

Sacred space is about creating a specific area for meditation, yoga, reading a book, or working on art of some form. The reason for having this sacred space is because it is very important that you have a place of complete peace. Peace of the mind, the body, and the spirit. It is a place where the worries and thoughts of the day or even just plain life are released. It is a meditation of the self that is very important for healing and growth.

Creating your space

While creating your space, whether it is inside or outside, think of the things that make you feel peace and happiness. Those are the things you will use to create your space. You can use things such as plants, water fountains, relaxing music, candles, altars, art, pictures of gardens, and other inspirational things that put you in a positive peaceful state.

It is important to remind others who are around you that this is your time for yourself. Ask them in a kind way to please allow you this time for yourself.

Do not allow clutter to invade your sacred space. Clutter creates frustration and it becomes very hard to clear your mind. Remember, "Clutter" is the opposite of "Space". You are creating space, your "sacred space".

The following are a few examples of sacred spaces:

1. A window facing peaceful scenery, flowers on the window seal, a little table and chair, and a pen and paper to write down things that you are grateful for. Add some peaceful music and you will have a basic yet very effective sacred space and moment.
2. A rug with a small table (close to the ground), with a candle that is lit and burning incense. Sit on the rug while your eyes are closed and the music is playing. The music will guide you through a journey of peace.
3. Lay down a blanket and sit on a patch of grass outside in a field. Lie down or sit up and breathe in the view of all the magical events that are happening right before your eyes. There is always life going happening around you. The trees are blowing in the wind, there are people walking by, two lovers are kissing, or even the birds flying above. This is an affirmation of the moment and a connection to life. You are being in the "in the present moment", and this is a powerful movement towards a positive life.

At the beginning of everything that exists, everything was intertwined (the big bang theory before explosion). Therefore, we are all still connected to everything. That feeling of connection will bring you peace. Peace to your soul and being. Sounds crazy yes, but very effective. You are not alone or separate. Everything and everyone is connected.

No one is connected in a way where they can directly control others, but all humans influence other human beings thoughts due to the fact that everything is connected by a frequency wave. Just like a wave in the ocean, an action begins with a suggestion by one and flows to others for them to choose their next action. Everyone influences everyone that they come in contact with. It is a ripple effect and each individual's separate choice allows us our individual response.

In conclusion . . .

Your sacred space reconnects you with yourself, the moment, a higher power, your purpose, and everything that is the right path for you. Most people don't know what they want because they do not calm their mind enough to figure it out. If you don't calm your mind and figure out what you truly want on your journey in this life, you then conform out of laziness and miss out on your true passion in this life. Use these tools to reconnect with what is yours. Build your sacred space and use it for your peace. It could save your life.

Positive Thinking

Positive thinking is a funny thing. Its funny how people tend to think that one thin layer of positivity deserves the "ultimate" response, but really is just a short lived band aid. One must continuously work at positivity and make it a habitual way of life. You can't build a relationship with less than few short moments and expect it to become a strong bond instantaneously. Same thing goes with positive thinking. It is a process that when you put time and effort you get life lasting results. This is so important in the human experience.

People will test you. They can be negative and make you feel like you are wrong. Just remember that you do not have to allow that to be part of your experience. People are naturally happy and the only reason they seem otherwise is because they have been conditioned or "programmed" due to depression and second guessing themselves. They have been conditioned and programmed to worry, be fearful, and fight everything in their lives from the time they were a child.

What if instead you spent your time loving and letting love engulf your soul so much that it enriches your life?

There is a new way of thinking. Don't waste your time fighting. Spend your time loving.

When a child becomes conditioned to be like their parents or the rest of the world they adapt to these ways because the child is learning its new world. This is why the world becomes so difficult to change. We are still living on the words and thoughts of our fathers and mothers. We are so guided to become what we are told to become because we are taught by people we love, trust to show us the way, and are afraid to be something more or different. Unfortunately we get lazy and adapt.

It is a massive process that not many people understand or can change overnight, but it is the rate of human evolution. What humans need to understand is if this is the rate, we need more love and understanding for one another. We need to understand that every other human being feels fear or love. If the entire universe was entangled at one moment and then it busted out making galaxies we are as close to each other as two cells that just performed the division process. How can one be separate from another? We are all one. We need to shed this illusion of separateness; separateness creates "dis-ease" (a body that is out of ease). We need a movement of unity. No more separateness. It does not serve us as a whole. Being positive and loving oneself is not only a helpful start, it serves the extension of you, and that is the rest of the world. Love thy self, thy neighbor, the rest of existence, and create a world that is holistic.

How? Use the gratitude list. Write down everything in this entire world you are grateful for.

Start small if you need to. Write down how grateful you are for yourself, your mate, your friends, your family, your town, your country, the people who fight for your country, your planet, the air you breathe, the fact you are ALIVE, and anything that comes to your mind. Remember, life could end in the next second. Life is a fragile precious moment that should be cherished. Why would any one small carbon unit (human), who is completely aware of itself and its direct surroundings, be so blind? The eyes are not needed to see. It is the heart that is used to feel. Feel the truth. Trust it. Move through life with it. Be guided with it and you will not lose. No matter what happens. Walk by unwavering faith and in the matrix you will glide like the butterfly in the wind.

Meditations

Before any meditation it is important to become aware of your surroundings, your posture, and your breath. Your surroundings must be peaceful and enable you to focus on calming the mind. Your posture is important because if you sit straight up with correct posture it allows the breath to flow through the body effortlessly. Proper breathing in and out at a steady, smooth, yet slow pace allows the breath in, and aids in the creativity of peaceful meditation. Focusing on your breathing while performing any meditation can also help with keeping your every day thoughts and feelings from interrupting your meditation. Remember this with any meditation and you will have a successful one.

The Healing Meditation

Following the above instructions and once you are ready to begin meditation, close your eyes and visualize a green glowing light/healing spirit that begins in the frontal lobe or your third eye (the invisible eye which provides perception beyond ordinary sight). The green light represents the breath and the connection of man to earth. The frontal lobe (third eye/sixth chakra) regulates emotional thoughts. You want to be mindful of your breath, connection to the earth, and bring forth the emotion of love and unwavering faith into your meditation to bring it its power (as if the emotion is the flicker that ignites the electricity and turns the light on in a room).

In the direction towards the "dis-eased" area of the body (place where the body is not at ease), visualize the green light/healing spirit moving from your frontal lobe. With every breath in as a movement forward and then every breath out releasing the negative energy that has penetrated your body (actually visualize waste leaving the body). It is a cleansing action, releasing negative waste from your body. Remember that steady breathing is the force that moves the healing spirit/green glowing light through the body to heal itself.

While this movement occurs say to yourself (inner or outer voice) "thank you for my healing" and really feel the emotion of gratitude for it. This emotional response brings forth the feeling of as if it were already so.

Continue all of this until the light has reached the area in need of healing. When the area is reached visualize the entire area getting so bright that it becomes a huge bright white light. Then visualize engulfing the entire area of white light until it becomes dimmer, dimmer, and disappears.

Slowly open your eyes and continue throughout your conscious day being thankful for your healing. REALLY feel it inside as if you have just witnessed an incredible miracle of healing, and it has happened from within you.

It is suggested to do this twice a day (when you wake and before you sleep at night).

The Instant State of Joy Meditation

Ever get really frustrated and wish your could pull yourself out of a negative feeling instantly? You can. But, first before anything you have to believe you can. You have to believe that there are things you can sit and think about and feel good about to change your experience instantly. It is all about focusing on positive triggers (that are your own and not triggers that make others happy).

Sit down and write down three things that you love and are passionate about. It is important to write down at least three so that you can rotate ideas and never get tired of just the one. These triggers will be the focal point of your meditation. Usually if one of your triggers is a project you could have a flicker of an idea on how to move forward in the project.

Next, write down on a piece of paper (until they are memorized completely), these three triggers. Carry it with you always.

When you have a moment that you feel stressed in any way pull it out, take slow deep breathes, and focus only on one of these things. Do not think about what is stressing you; only think about this one positive trigger that will bring your heart to a positive frequency and change your emotional vibration.

Remember to keep breathing slowly in and out while doing this. It is so important to remember this because it helps with bringing the emotional vibration to that positive frequency. It changes the rate of your heart and your heart is the largest frequency unity in your human body. It tells the body what to do.

When you feel a change in your emotions from a raised negative heart rate to a steady positive disposition, you are now free to continue with your day. You are free to move forward knowing that situations do not determine your experience. You determine your experience and you alone.

Notes

Biannual Intentions

1.

2.

3.

4.

5.

6.

7.

8.

9.

10.

11.

12.

Gratitude List

1.

2.

3.

4.

5.

6.

<u>Gratitude List</u>

1.

2.

3.

4.

5.

6.

Gratitude List

1.

2.

3.

4.

5.

6.

Gratitude List

1.

2.

3.

4.

5.

6.

Gratitude List

1.

2.

3.

4.

5.

6.

Gratitude List

1.

2.

3.

4.

5.

6.

Gratitude List

1.

2.

3.

4.

5.

6.

Gratitude List

1.

2.

3.

4.

5.

6.

Gratitude List

1.

2.

3.

4.

5.

6.

Gratitude List

1.

2.

3.

4.

5.

6.

Gratitude List

1.

2.

3.

4.

5.

6.

Gratitude List

1.

2.

3.

4.

5.

6.

Daily Life Planner

Morning

8am

9am

10am

11am

12pm Noon

1pm

2pm

3pm

4pm

Evening

5pm

6pm

Daily Life Planner

Morning

8am

9am

10am

11am

12pm Noon

1pm

2pm

3pm

4pm

Evening

5pm

6pm

Daily Life Planner

Morning

8am

9am

10am

11am

12pm Noon

1pm

2pm

3pm

4pm

Evening

5pm

6pm

Daily Life Planner

Morning

8am

9am

10am

11am

12pm Noon

1pm

2pm

3pm

4pm

Evening

5pm

6pm

Daily Life Planner

Morning

8am

9am

10am

11am

12pm Noon

1pm

2pm

3pm

4pm

Evening

5pm

6pm

Daily Life Planner

Morning

8am

9am

10am

11am

12pm Noon

1pm

2pm

3pm

4pm

Evening

5pm

6pm

Daily Life Planner

Morning

8am

9am

10am

11am

12pm Noon

1pm

2pm

3pm

4pm

Evening

5pm

6pm

Daily Life Planner

Morning

8am

9am

10am

11am

12pm Noon

1pm

2pm

3pm

4pm

Evening

5pm

6pm

Daily Life Planner

Morning

8am

9am

10am

11am

12pm Noon

1pm

2pm

3pm

4pm

Evening

5pm

6pm

Daily Life Planner

Morning

8am

9am

10am

11am

12pm Noon

1pm

2pm

3pm

4pm

Evening

5pm

6pm

Daily Life Planner

Morning

8am

9am

10am

11am

12pm Noon

1pm

2pm

3pm

4pm

Evening

5pm

6pm

Daily Life Planner

Morning

8am

9am

10am

11am

12pm Noon

1pm

2pm

3pm

4pm

Evening

5pm

6pm

Daily Life Planner

Morning

8am

9am

10am

11am

12pm Noon

1pm

2pm

3pm

4pm

Evening

5pm

6pm

Daily Life Planner

Morning

8am

9am

10am

11am

12pm Noon

1pm

2pm

3pm

4pm

Evening

5pm

6pm

Daily Life Planner

Morning

8am

9am

10am

11am

12pm Noon

1pm

2pm

3pm

4pm

Evening

5pm

6pm

Daily Life Planner

Morning

8am

9am

10am

11am

12pm Noon

1pm

2pm

3pm

4pm

Evening

5pm

6pm

Daily Life Planner

Morning

8am

9am

10am

11am

12pm Noon

1pm

2pm

3pm

4pm

Evening

5pm

6pm

Daily Life Planner

Morning

8am

9am

10am

11am

12pm Noon

1pm

2pm

3pm

4pm

Evening

5pm

6pm

Daily Life Planner

Morning

8am

9am

10am

11am

12pm Noon

1pm

2pm

3pm

4pm

Evening

5pm

6pm

Daily Life Planner

Morning

8am

9am

10am

11am

12pm Noon

1pm

2pm

3pm

4pm

Evening

5pm

6pm

Daily Life Planner

Morning

8am

9am

10am

11am

12pm Noon

1pm

2pm

3pm

4pm

Evening

5pm

6pm

Daily Life Planner

Morning

8am

9am

10am

11am

12pm Noon

1pm

2pm

3pm

4pm

Evening

5pm

6pm

Daily Life Planner

Morning

8am

9am

10am

11am

12pm Noon

1pm

2pm

3pm

4pm

Evening

5pm

6pm

Daily Life Planner

Morning

8am

9am

10am

11am

12pm Noon

1pm

2pm

3pm

4pm

Evening

5pm

6pm

Daily Life Planner

Morning

8am

9am

10am

11am

12pm Noon

1pm

2pm

3pm

4pm

Evening

5pm

6pm

Daily Life Planner

Morning

8am

9am

10am

11am

12pm Noon

1pm

2pm

3pm

4pm

Evening

5pm

6pm

Daily Life Planner

Morning

8am

9am

10am

11am

12pm Noon

1pm

2pm

3pm

4pm

Evening

5pm

6pm

Daily Life Planner

Morning

8am

9am

10am

11am

12pm Noon

1pm

2pm

3pm

4pm

Evening

5pm

6pm

Daily Life Planner

Morning

8am

9am

10am

11am

12pm Noon

1pm

2pm

3pm

4pm

Evening

5pm

6pm

Daily Life Planner

Morning

8am

9am

10am

11am

12pm Noon

1pm

2pm

3pm

4pm

Evening

5pm

6pm

Daily Life Planner

Morning

8am

9am

10am

11am

12pm Noon

1pm

2pm

3pm

4pm

Evening

5pm

6pm

Daily Life Planner

Morning

8am

9am

10am

11am

12pm Noon

1pm

2pm

3pm

4pm

Evening

5pm

6pm

Daily Life Planner

Morning

8am

9am

10am

11am

12pm Noon

1pm

2pm

3pm

4pm

Evening

5pm

6pm

Daily Life Planner

Morning

8am

9am

10am

11am

12pm Noon

1pm

2pm

3pm

4pm

Evening

5pm

6pm

Daily Life Planner

Morning

8am

9am

10am

11am

12pm Noon

1pm

2pm

3pm

4pm

Evening

5pm

6pm

Daily Life Planner

Morning

8am

9am

10am

11am

12pm Noon

1pm

2pm

3pm

4pm

Evening

5pm

6pm

Daily Life Planner

Morning

8am

9am

10am

11am

12pm Noon

1pm

2pm

3pm

4pm

Evening

5pm

6pm

Daily Life Planner

Morning

8am

9am

10am

11am

12pm Noon

1pm

2pm

3pm

4pm

Evening

5pm

6pm

Daily Life Planner

Morning

8am

9am

10am

11am

12pm Noon

1pm

2pm

3pm

4pm

Evening

5pm

6pm

Daily Life Planner

Morning

8am

9am

10am

11am

12pm Noon

1pm

2pm

3pm

4pm

Evening

5pm

6pm

Daily Life Planner

Morning

8am

9am

10am

11am

12pm Noon

1pm

2pm

3pm

4pm

Evening

5pm

6pm

Daily Life Planner

Morning

8am

9am

10am

11am

12pm Noon

1pm

2pm

3pm

4pm

Evening

5pm

6pm

Daily Life Planner

Morning

8am

9am

10am

11am

12pm Noon

1pm

2pm

3pm

4pm

Evening

5pm

6pm

Daily Life Planner

Morning

8am

9am

10am

11am

12pm Noon

1pm

2pm

3pm

4pm

Evening

5pm

6pm

Daily Life Planner

Morning

8am

9am

10am

11am

12pm Noon

1pm

2pm

3pm

4pm

Evening

5pm

6pm

Daily Life Planner

Morning

8am

9am

10am

11am

12pm Noon

1pm

2pm

3pm

4pm

Evening

5pm

6pm

Daily Life Planner

Morning

8am

9am

10am

11am

12pm Noon

1pm

2pm

3pm

4pm

Evening

5pm

6pm

Daily Life Planner

Morning

8am

9am

10am

11am

12pm Noon

1pm

2pm

3pm

4pm

Evening

5pm

6pm

Daily Life Planner

Morning

8am

9am

10am

11am

12pm Noon

1pm

2pm

3pm

4pm

Evening

5pm

6pm

Daily Life Planner

Morning

8am

9am

10am

11am

12pm Noon

1pm

2pm

3pm

4pm

Evening

5pm

6pm

Daily Life Planner

Morning

8am

9am

10am

11am

12pm Noon

1pm

2pm

3pm

4pm

Evening

5pm

6pm

Daily Life Planner

Morning

8am

9am

10am

11am

12pm Noon

1pm

2pm

3pm

4pm

Evening

5pm

6pm

Daily Life Planner

Morning

8am

9am

10am

11am

12pm Noon

1pm

2pm

3pm

4pm

Evening

5pm

6pm

Daily Life Planner

Morning

8am

9am

10am

11am

12pm Noon

1pm

2pm

3pm

4pm

Evening

5pm

6pm

Daily Life Planner

Morning

8am

9am

10am

11am

12pm Noon

1pm

2pm

3pm

4pm

Evening

5pm

6pm

Daily Life Planner

Morning

8am

9am

10am

11am

12pm Noon

1pm

2pm

3pm

4pm

Evening

5pm

6pm

Daily Life Planner

Morning

8am

9am

10am

11am

12pm Noon

1pm

2pm

3pm

4pm

Evening

5pm

6pm

Daily Life Planner

Morning

8am

9am

10am

11am

12pm Noon

1pm

2pm

3pm

4pm

Evening

5pm

6pm

Daily Life Planner

Morning

8am

9am

10am

11am

12pm Noon

1pm

2pm

3pm

4pm

Evening

5pm

6pm

Daily Life Planner

Morning

8am

9am

10am

11am

12pm Noon

1pm

2pm

3pm

4pm

Evening

5pm

6pm

Daily Life Planner

Morning

8am

9am

10am

11am

12pm Noon

1pm

2pm

3pm

4pm

Evening

5pm

6pm

Daily Life Planner

Morning

8am

9am

10am

11am

12pm Noon

1pm

2pm

3pm

4pm

Evening

5pm

6pm

Daily Life Planner

Morning

8am

9am

10am

11am

12pm Noon

1pm

2pm

3pm

4pm

Evening

5pm

6pm

Daily Life Planner

Morning

8am

9am

10am

11am

12pm Noon

1pm

2pm

3pm

4pm

Evening

5pm

6pm

Daily Life Planner

Morning

8am

9am

10am

11am

12pm Noon

1pm

2pm

3pm

4pm

Evening

5pm

6pm

Daily Life Planner

Morning

8am

9am

10am

11am

12pm Noon

1pm

2pm

3pm

4pm

Evening

5pm

6pm

Daily Life Planner

Morning

8am

9am

10am

11am

12pm Noon

1pm

2pm

3pm

4pm

Evening

5pm

6pm

Daily Life Planner

Morning

8am

9am

10am

11am

12pm Noon

1pm

2pm

3pm

4pm

Evening

5pm

6pm

Daily Life Planner

Morning

8am

9am

10am

11am

12pm Noon

1pm

2pm

3pm

4pm

Evening

5pm

6pm

Daily Life Planner

Morning

8am

9am

10am

11am

12pm Noon

1pm

2pm

3pm

4pm

Evening

5pm

6pm

Daily Life Planner

Morning

8am

9am

10am

11am

12pm Noon

1pm

2pm

3pm

4pm

Evening

5pm

6pm

Daily Life Planner

Morning

8am

9am

10am

11am

12pm Noon

1pm

2pm

3pm

4pm

Evening

5pm

6pm

Daily Life Planner

Morning

8am

9am

10am

11am

12pm Noon

1pm

2pm

3pm

4pm

Evening

5pm

6pm

Daily Life Planner

Morning

8am

9am

10am

11am

12pm Noon

1pm

2pm

3pm

4pm

Evening

5pm

6pm

Daily Life Planner

Morning

8am

9am

10am

11am

12pm Noon

1pm

2pm

3pm

4pm

Evening

5pm

6pm

Daily Life Planner

Morning

8am

9am

10am

11am

12pm Noon

1pm

2pm

3pm

4pm

Evening

5pm

6pm

Daily Life Planner

Morning

8am

9am

10am

11am

12pm Noon

1pm

2pm

3pm

4pm

Evening

5pm

6pm

Daily Life Planner

Morning

8am

9am

10am

11am

12pm Noon

1pm

2pm

3pm

4pm

Evening

5pm

6pm

Daily Life Planner

Morning

8am

9am

10am

11am

12pm Noon

1pm

2pm

3pm

4pm

Evening

5pm

6pm

Daily Life Planner

Morning

8am

9am

10am

11am

12pm Noon

1pm

2pm

3pm

4pm

Evening

5pm

6pm

Daily Life Planner

Morning

8am

9am

10am

11am

12pm Noon

1pm

2pm

3pm

4pm

Evening

5pm

6pm

Daily Life Planner

Morning

8am

9am

10am

11am

12pm Noon

1pm

2pm

3pm

4pm

Evening

5pm

6pm

Daily Life Planner

Morning

8am

9am

10am

11am

12pm Noon

1pm

2pm

3pm

4pm

Evening

5pm

6pm

Daily Life Planner

Morning

8am

9am

10am

11am

12pm Noon

1pm

2pm

3pm

4pm

Evening

5pm

6pm

Daily Life Planner

Morning

8am

9am

10am

11am

12pm Noon

1pm

2pm

3pm

4pm

Evening

5pm

6pm

Daily Life Planner

Morning

8am

9am

10am

11am

12pm Noon

1pm

2pm

3pm

4pm

Evening

5pm

6pm

Daily Life Planner

Morning

8am

9am

10am

11am

12pm Noon

1pm

2pm

3pm

4pm

Evening

5pm

6pm

Daily Life Planner

Morning

8am

9am

10am

11am

12pm Noon

1pm

2pm

3pm

4pm

Evening

5pm

6pm

Daily Life Planner

Morning

8am

9am

10am

11am

12pm Noon

1pm

2pm

3pm

4pm

Evening

5pm

6pm

Daily Life Planner

Morning

8am

9am

10am

11am

12pm Noon

1pm

2pm

3pm

4pm

Evening

5pm

6pm

Daily Life Planner

Morning

8am

9am

10am

11am

12pm Noon

1pm

2pm

3pm

4pm

Evening

5pm

6pm

Daily Life Planner

Morning

8am

9am

10am

11am

12pm Noon

1pm

2pm

3pm

4pm

Evening

5pm

6pm

Daily Life Planner

Morning

8am

9am

10am

11am

12pm Noon

1pm

2pm

3pm

4pm

Evening

5pm

6pm

Daily Life Planner

Morning

8am

9am

10am

11am

12pm Noon

1pm

2pm

3pm

4pm

Evening

5pm

6pm

Daily Life Planner

Morning

8am

9am

10am

11am

12pm Noon

1pm

2pm

3pm

4pm

Evening

5pm

6pm

Daily Life Planner

Morning

8am

9am

10am

11am

12pm Noon

1pm

2pm

3pm

4pm

Evening

5pm

6pm

Daily Life Planner

Morning

8am

9am

10am

11am

12pm Noon

1pm

2pm

3pm

4pm

Evening

5pm

6pm

Daily Life Planner

Morning

8am

9am

10am

11am

12pm Noon

1pm

2pm

3pm

4pm

Evening

5pm

6pm

Daily Life Planner

Morning

8am

9am

10am

11am

12pm Noon

1pm

2pm

3pm

4pm

Evening

5pm

6pm

Daily Life Planner

Morning

8am

9am

10am

11am

12pm Noon

1pm

2pm

3pm

4pm

Evening

5pm

6pm

Daily Life Planner

Morning

8am

9am

10am

11am

12pm Noon

1pm

2pm

3pm

4pm

Evening

5pm

6pm

Daily Life Planner

Morning

8am

9am

10am

11am

12pm Noon

1pm

2pm

3pm

4pm

Evening

5pm

6pm

Daily Life Planner

Morning

8am

9am

10am

11am

12pm Noon

1pm

2pm

3pm

4pm

Evening

5pm

6pm

Daily Life Planner

Morning

8am

9am

10am

11am

12pm Noon

1pm

2pm

3pm

4pm

Evening

5pm

6pm

Daily Life Planner

Morning

8am

9am

10am

11am

12pm Noon

1pm

2pm

3pm

4pm

Evening

5pm

6pm

Daily Life Planner

Morning

8am

9am

10am

11am

12pm Noon

1pm

2pm

3pm

4pm

Evening

5pm

6pm

Daily Life Planner

Morning

8am

9am

10am

11am

12pm Noon

1pm

2pm

3pm

4pm

Evening

5pm

6pm

Daily Life Planner

Morning

8am

9am

10am

11am

12pm Noon

1pm

2pm

3pm

4pm

Evening

5pm

6pm

Daily Life Planner

Morning

8am

9am

10am

11am

12pm Noon

1pm

2pm

3pm

4pm

Evening

5pm

6pm

Daily Life Planner

Morning

8am

9am

10am

11am

12pm Noon

1pm

2pm

3pm

4pm

Evening

5pm

6pm

Daily Life Planner

Morning

8am

9am

10am

11am

12pm Noon

1pm

2pm

3pm

4pm

Evening

5pm

6pm

Daily Life Planner

Morning

8am

9am

10am

11am

12pm Noon

1pm

2pm

3pm

4pm

Evening

5pm

6pm

Daily Life Planner

Morning

8am

9am

10am

11am

12pm Noon

1pm

2pm

3pm

4pm

Evening

5pm

6pm

Daily Life Planner

Morning

8am

9am

10am

11am

12pm Noon

1pm

2pm

3pm

4pm

Evening

5pm

6pm

Daily Life Planner

Morning

8am

9am

10am

11am

12pm Noon

1pm

2pm

3pm

4pm

Evening

5pm

6pm

Daily Life Planner

Morning

8am

9am

10am

11am

12pm Noon

1pm

2pm

3pm

4pm

Evening

5pm

6pm

Daily Life Planner

Morning

8am

9am

10am

11am

12pm Noon

1pm

2pm

3pm

4pm

Evening

5pm

6pm

Daily Life Planner

Morning

8am

9am

10am

11am

12pm Noon

1pm

2pm

3pm

4pm

Evening

5pm

6pm

Daily Life Planner

Morning

8am

9am

10am

11am

12pm Noon

1pm

2pm

3pm

4pm

Evening

5pm

6pm

Daily Life Planner

Morning

8am

9am

10am

11am

12pm Noon

1pm

2pm

3pm

4pm

Evening

5pm

6pm

Daily Life Planner

Morning

8am

9am

10am

11am

12pm Noon

1pm

2pm

3pm

4pm

Evening

5pm

6pm

Daily Life Planner

Morning

8am

9am

10am

11am

12pm Noon

1pm

2pm

3pm

4pm

Evening

5pm

6pm

Daily Life Planner

Morning

8am

9am

10am

11am

12pm Noon

1pm

2pm

3pm

4pm

Evening

5pm

6pm

Daily Life Planner

Morning

8am

9am

10am

11am

12pm Noon

1pm

2pm

3pm

4pm

Evening

5pm

6pm

Daily Life Planner

Morning

8am

9am

10am

11am

12pm Noon

1pm

2pm

3pm

4pm

Evening

5pm

6pm

Daily Life Planner

Morning

8am

9am

10am

11am

12pm Noon

1pm

2pm

3pm

4pm

Evening

5pm

6pm

Daily Life Planner

Morning

8am

9am

10am

11am

12pm Noon

1pm

2pm

3pm

4pm

Evening

5pm

6pm

Daily Life Planner

Morning

8am

9am

10am

11am

12pm Noon

1pm

2pm

3pm

4pm

Evening

5pm

6pm

Daily Life Planner

Morning

8am

9am

10am

11am

12pm Noon

1pm

2pm

3pm

4pm

Evening

5pm

6pm

Daily Life Planner

Morning

8am

9am

10am

11am

12pm Noon

1pm

2pm

3pm

4pm

Evening

5pm

6pm

Daily Life Planner

Morning

8am

9am

10am

11am

12pm Noon

1pm

2pm

3pm

4pm

Evening

5pm

6pm

<u>Daily Life Planner</u>

Morning

8am

9am

10am

11am

12pm Noon

1pm

2pm

3pm

4pm

Evening

5pm

6pm

Daily Life Planner

Morning

8am

9am

10am

11am

12pm Noon

1pm

2pm

3pm

4pm

Evening

5pm

6pm

Daily Life Planner

Morning

8am

9am

10am

11am

12pm Noon

1pm

2pm

3pm

4pm

Evening

5pm

6pm

Daily Life Planner

Morning

8am

9am

10am

11am

12pm Noon

1pm

2pm

3pm

4pm

Evening

5pm

6pm

Daily Life Planner

Morning

8am

9am

10am

11am

12pm Noon

1pm

2pm

3pm

4pm

Evening

5pm

6pm

Daily Life Planner

Morning

8am

9am

10am

11am

12pm Noon

1pm

2pm

3pm

4pm

Evening

5pm

6pm

Daily Life Planner

Morning

8am

9am

10am

11am

12pm Noon

1pm

2pm

3pm

4pm

Evening

5pm

6pm

Daily Life Planner

Morning

8am

9am

10am

11am

12pm Noon

1pm

2pm

3pm

4pm

Evening

5pm

6pm

<u>Daily Life Planner</u>

Morning

8am

9am

10am

11am

12pm Noon

1pm

2pm

3pm

4pm

Evening

5pm

6pm

Daily Life Planner

Morning

8am

9am

10am

11am

12pm Noon

1pm

2pm

3pm

4pm

Evening

5pm

6pm

Daily Life Planner

Morning

8am

9am

10am

11am

12pm Noon

1pm

2pm

3pm

4pm

Evening

5pm

6pm

Daily Life Planner

Morning

8am

9am

10am

11am

12pm Noon

1pm

2pm

3pm

4pm

Evening

5pm

6pm

Daily Life Planner

Morning

8am

9am

10am

11am

12pm Noon

1pm

2pm

3pm

4pm

Evening

5pm

6pm

Daily Life Planner

Morning

8am

9am

10am

11am

12pm Noon

1pm

2pm

3pm

4pm

Evening

5pm

6pm

Daily Life Planner

Morning

8am

9am

10am

11am

12pm Noon

1pm

2pm

3pm

4pm

Evening

5pm

6pm

Daily Life Planner

Morning

8am

9am

10am

11am

12pm Noon

1pm

2pm

3pm

4pm

Evening

5pm

6pm

Daily Life Planner

Morning

8am

9am

10am

11am

12pm Noon

1pm

2pm

3pm

4pm

Evening

5pm

6pm

Daily Life Planner

Morning

8am

9am

10am

11am

12pm Noon

1pm

2pm

3pm

4pm

Evening

5pm

6pm

Daily Life Planner

Morning

8am

9am

10am

11am

12pm Noon

1pm

2pm

3pm

4pm

Evening

5pm

6pm

Daily Life Planner

Morning

8am

9am

10am

11am

12pm Noon

1pm

2pm

3pm

4pm

Evening

5pm

6pm

Daily Life Planner

Morning

8am

9am

10am

11am

12pm Noon

1pm

2pm

3pm

4pm

Evening

5pm

6pm

Daily Life Planner

Morning

8am

9am

10am

11am

12pm Noon

1pm

2pm

3pm

4pm

Evening

5pm

6pm

Daily Life Planner

Morning

8am

9am

10am

11am

12pm Noon

1pm

2pm

3pm

4pm

Evening

5pm

6pm

Daily Life Planner

Morning

8am

9am

10am

11am

12pm Noon

1pm

2pm

3pm

4pm

Evening

5pm

6pm

Daily Life Planner

Morning

8am

9am

10am

11am

12pm Noon

1pm

2pm

3pm

4pm

Evening

5pm

6pm

Daily Life Planner

Morning

8am

9am

10am

11am

12pm Noon

1pm

2pm

3pm

4pm

Evening

5pm

6pm

Daily Life Planner

Morning

8am

9am

10am

11am

12pm Noon

1pm

2pm

3pm

4pm

Evening

5pm

6pm

Daily Life Planner

Morning

8am

9am

10am

11am

12pm Noon

1pm

2pm

3pm

4pm

Evening

5pm

6pm

Daily Life Planner

Morning

8am

9am

10am

11am

12pm Noon

1pm

2pm

3pm

4pm

Evening

5pm

6pm

Daily Life Planner

Morning

8am

9am

10am

11am

12pm Noon

1pm

2pm

3pm

4pm

Evening

5pm

6pm

Daily Life Planner

Morning

8am

9am

10am

11am

12pm Noon

1pm

2pm

3pm

4pm

Evening

5pm

6pm

Daily Life Planner

Morning

8am

9am

10am

11am

12pm Noon

1pm

2pm

3pm

4pm

Evening

5pm

6pm

Daily Life Planner

Morning

8am

9am

10am

11am

12pm Noon

1pm

2pm

3pm

4pm

Evening

5pm

6pm

Daily Life Planner

Morning

8am

9am

10am

11am

12pm Noon

1pm

2pm

3pm

4pm

Evening

5pm

6pm

Daily Life Planner

Morning

8am

9am

10am

11am

12pm Noon

1pm

2pm

3pm

4pm

Evening

5pm

6pm

Daily Life Planner

Morning

8am

9am

10am

11am

12pm Noon

1pm

2pm

3pm

4pm

Evening

5pm

6pm

Daily Life Planner

Morning

8am

9am

10am

11am

12pm Noon

1pm

2pm

3pm

4pm

Evening

5pm

6pm

Daily Life Planner

Morning

8am

9am

10am

11am

12pm Noon

1pm

2pm

3pm

4pm

Evening

5pm

6pm

Daily Life Planner

Morning

8am

9am

10am

11am

12pm Noon

1pm

2pm

3pm

4pm

Evening

5pm

6pm

Daily Life Planner

Morning

8am

9am

10am

11am

12pm Noon

1pm

2pm

3pm

4pm

Evening

5pm

6pm

Daily Life Planner

Morning

8am

9am

10am

11am

12pm Noon

1pm

2pm

3pm

4pm

Evening

5pm

6pm

Daily Life Planner

Morning

8am

9am

10am

11am

12pm Noon

1pm

2pm

3pm

4pm

Evening

5pm

6pm

Daily Life Planner

Morning

8am

9am

10am

11am

12pm Noon

1pm

2pm

3pm

4pm

Evening

5pm

6pm

Daily Life Planner

Morning

8am

9am

10am

11am

12pm Noon

1pm

2pm

3pm

4pm

Evening

5pm

6pm

Daily Life Planner

Morning

8am

9am

10am

11am

12pm Noon

1pm

2pm

3pm

4pm

Evening

5pm

6pm

Daily Life Planner

Morning

8am

9am

10am

11am

12pm Noon

1pm

2pm

3pm

4pm

Evening

5pm

6pm

Daily Life Planner

Morning

8am

9am

10am

11am

12pm Noon

1pm

2pm

3pm

4pm

Evening

5pm

6pm

Daily Life Planner

Morning

8am

9am

10am

11am

12pm Noon

1pm

2pm

3pm

4pm

Evening

5pm

6pm

Daily Life Planner

Morning

8am

9am

10am

11am

12pm Noon

1pm

2pm

3pm

4pm

Evening

5pm

6pm

Daily Life Planner

Morning

8am

9am

10am

11am

12pm Noon

1pm

2pm

3pm

4pm

Evening

5pm

6pm

Daily Life Planner

Morning

8am

9am

10am

11am

12pm Noon

1pm

2pm

3pm

4pm

Evening

5pm

6pm

Daily Life Planner

Morning

8am

9am

10am

11am

12pm Noon

1pm

2pm

3pm

4pm

Evening

5pm

6pm

Daily Life Planner

Morning

8am

9am

10am

11am

12pm Noon

1pm

2pm

3pm

4pm

Evening

5pm

6pm

Daily Life Planner

Morning

8am

9am

10am

11am

12pm Noon

1pm

2pm

3pm

4pm

Evening

5pm

6pm

Daily Life Planner

Morning

8am

9am

10am

11am

12pm Noon

1pm

2pm

3pm

4pm

Evening

5pm

6pm

Daily Life Planner

Morning

8am

9am

10am

11am

12pm Noon

1pm

2pm

3pm

4pm

Evening

5pm

6pm

Epilogue

Other helpful ideas!

If you are more of a "visual" individual create visual aids that will help remind you of your goals, dreams, and aspirations! One great idea is creating a "Boom Board". What is a Boom Board you ask? A Boom Board is a large 30x20 cardboard or poster board along with cut out pictures from magazines, pictures, postcards, or even just words that you can look at every single day and focus on what you want out of this life time.

Another great idea is erasable markers! Yes, erasable markers are great little tools that allow you to write positive affirmations on your bathroom mirror, closet mirror, or on dry erase coating on your wall. There is now a type of paint called "dry erase coating" that allows you to turn your wall into a dry erase board. It works wonders!

Whatever little creative idea you may use it is important to remind yourself that this is a "positive" journey you have decided to place yourself on. It is the journey that brings us happiness and not the destination, so bring more happiness into your journey.

Author Biography/About the Author:

Angela Gerber has practiced healing humans as an Aesthetician and rescued animals upon adoption for many years. Studying Reiki; healing has been Angela's passion throughout her life. Gerber lives with her husband and three dogs in Las Vegas, Nevada while building her career as an author, healer, and a life coach.

Angela is also the creator of www.ButterflyEffect-Meditation.com; Butterfly's community of life meditations and easy to understand interpretation of meditation techniques.